# Dedication

For entrepreneurial spirits everywhere.

It is hoped that this book becomes a help for whatever you, the reader, need.

# How Not to Lose Your Bass in Business

## Business is Like Fishing

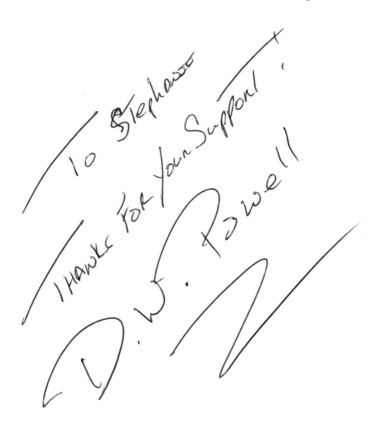

To Stephanie
Thanks For Your Support!
D. W. Powell

# How Not to Lose Your Bass in Business

*Business is Like Fishing*

## D.W. POWELL

**DocUmeant** *Publishing*
244 5th Avenue
Suite G-200
NY, NY 10001
646-233-4366
www.DocUmeantPublishing.com

# How Not to Lose Your Bass in Business
## *Business is Like Fishing*

**Published by**
DocUmeant Publishing
244 5th Avenue, Suite G-200
NY, NY 10001
Phone: 646-233-4366

**Illustrator,** Beverly Womack

**Copy Editor,** Philip S Marks

**Cover Design & Layout,** DocUmeant Designs

Second Edition

ISBN13: 978-1-937801-51-9
ISBN10: 1-937801-51-9

# Contents

# Foreword

Dick has written a clever parable to explain and
embrace the principles of successful enterprise and
rewarding living. Those principles, when learned
young and practiced throughout one's life, lead to
rewards in all areas of living: at home, with one's
family, and in whatever career you should choose.
It particularly pertains to entrepreneurship, which
is the basis of our wonderful nation, the USA.

Dick's common sense approach, grown out of his
life experiences, his faith, and upbringing remind
me of my dad, who with an eighth grade education and on-the-job training, was able to run two
successful businesses, support and educate his

family, and live a happy middle-class life. Hard work, long hours, and dedication to the job at hand, treating customer right, knowing your limits, and following through with your promises are all necessary for business success. A college degree is not necessary to attain these characteristics. Depending on your goals, as much education as you can afford is recommended. But, education without the basic life principles that Dick presents in this book will not necessarily lead to success in business.

Honesty, integrity, keeping your word, persistence, and following through (delivering) are all necessary for a successful business. I have known Dick Powell for many years and know that he personally has these characteristics. Listen to him!

*H. James Free, M.D.*

# Note from the Author

I have studied business for well over forty years and leadership even longer. Growing up in a small town where Scouting was a large part of being a youth, I discovered that leaders used words that made a difference. As an adult, I spent time in the corporate world growing from the lowest of the low, a grunt lineman for the telephone company, to the height of my corporate career as the interim director of instruction and training for a large corporation. I grew to understand that owning my own business was what I wanted to do.

As I acquired an understanding of how business works, I learned that leadership was the driving force behind it. I had worked for many managers in my life—but only a few leaders. Some were good, one was great, and there is a list of personalities I never want to be like.

As an outdoor person, I realized that the professional fishing people I met had it all together and I should listen and learn from them.

The old way of a "handshake was a bond" between two people is still strong. Now, in today's world, we need to take the time to build relationships with people we know, like, and trust so we can return to doing what is right because it is the right thing to do.

# Introduction

This book is a "Lessons Learned book." Lessons learned from a normal, not so famous guy. I have never been on safari, won a gold medal, swum the English Channel, or climbed Mt. Everest.

I started out bagging groceries, fixing cars, digging ditches, driving huge trucks, climbing telephone poles, building companies, helping others realize and live their dreams, and raising a family with my wonderful wife for forty-two years, and counting.

If you want to graduate from digging ditches to owning your own company, this could be your starting point.

I have also included comments from Robin, my wife, who has been and is an active observer, partner, and now commentator in our wonderful life together.

## Robin's Rhetoric

*Dick and I met in Sunday school when we were twelve and thirteen. It was a small church, no real sanctuary, just a fellowship hall building with a few classrooms. Our class met in the kitchen. He was seldom in Sunday School but his family usually made it to church a few times a month. I found them entertaining. I thought he was cute. The church thought it was wonderful when the Powell Family joined because they had four children.*

*A few years later the church decided to start a Boy Scout troop. Dick's dad was a volunteer somewhere above the troop level, my dad was the only one who had been a Scout so he was a leader, and Dick transferred in as the Senior Patrol Leader. The SPL is the youth leader of the troop. He was pretty good at bossing the other Scouts around. Our family camped for a week two summers with the troop on the Withlacoochee River because the boys' families could not afford to send them to the local camp. The first summer we were fourteen and fifteen. I think Dick took a lot of teasing about the Scoutmaster's daughter and I had SUCH a crush I did not know whether to talk to him or find somewhere to go when he was in our area. He had a loud mouth and used it continuously. We always knew where Dick was and what he was thinking.*

*Although we lived in different areas, we started at the same high school the same year. I remember how hard it was walking into classrooms that first day and knowing no one except two boys I had gone to elementary and junior high with. At fifteen I was taller and a girl so they ignored me. The other students had their groups established, and I felt mostly invisible. What a shiny spot in my day those first weeks when I passed Dick in the hall and we smiled at each other. A friendly face and a hello! He knew even less people than I did in that student body of two thousand.*

*Eventually we had a date. Six months later we had a second date. Dick mentioned marriage, I was pretty sure it was just a line he was trying out. I had plans to go away for college after high school. My mom had different ideas. We were engaged at Christmas time my senior year of high school. Dick began a thirty year career with the phone company about the time I graduated. I started junior college the end of the summer and we married the next New Year's Day in the church where we met.*

*Throughout our marriage we have made decisions based on what was right for us at the time. According to our mothers, we were both independent children. We have had good friends throughout our lives but have been each other's best friends since 1971. Often we agree to disagree on things and that keeps life interesting. Sometimes it gets loud. We made some lifelong decisions on our honeymoon to do some things like one family or the other and mostly live our lives in ways that were right for us. So far, so good, through all of the ups, downs, and challenges, we never know what a new day will bring.*

*In retrospect, we have always thought things through, maybe did a bit of research, planned things, and did them as planned, shared ideas and information with others, celebrated the simple and momentous joys, evaluated how things went and how to improve the next thing. I used to say that anything was fun—once, and still enjoy new experiences.*

*This book is the result of Dick's passion to help people. The "Robin's Rhetoric" sections are simply my comments.*

# Section I

# CHAPTER 1

# Goin' Fishn'

*"I remind myself every morning: Nothing I say this day will teach me anything. So if I'm going to learn, I must do it by listening."* —**Larry King**

One late fall afternoon my wife and I were enjoying some time out in Orlando, Florida, at a beautiful condo overlooking a blue lake, with ducks and a water fountain. Her dream vacation is to read late into the night, sleep in late, enjoy her hot tea in the morning, sit by the pool to read and take in some sun time, and maybe in the afternoon do some shopping at an International Drive outlet mall.

My dream is about action on a different scale. It is all about going fishing. A day on the water, catching big fish, the adrenaline rush, having an adventure, that's what I need. All I could see was just one day gearing up and going after largemouth bass. I wanted to catch a trophy size largemouth bass. I needed a full day of fishing and then I would be able to go back to the condo with pictures, stories, and great memories.

I have learned from my past experiences fishing around the United States, the best way to enjoy a fishing trip in a new location is to hire a known fishing guide. I was looking for someone who knew the area and what bait and tackle to use. I was looking for a guide who could put me on to largemouth bass, someone who could fulfill my dream of a ten pounder.

I had done my homework before the trip. I had spent hours on the Internet and making phone calls, and I had the best of the best guide's phone number already saved in my cell phone.

I made some careful negotiations with my business partner and my wife, and then I placed the call.

The telephone rang and Sammy Bassman answered, "Good afternoon. This is Sammy Bassman, I guide—you catch! How may I be of service to you?"

I got excited and heard very little after the word *Bassman.* I knew this was the guy I needed to fish with. I asked as many questions of Sammy in the same way I would interview a person for a job in my company. We quickly settled on the price, what would be provided, how early I was to meet him, where and what I needed to bring with me.

He had his list ready and quickly gave me all the answers. Sammy said, "Bring yourself, a good attitude, a hat, sun screen, a camera, and be ready to have fun."

Sammy proceeded to ask if I preferred artificial bait or live shiners. I answered, "Live shiners."

Sammy's response was quick and deliberate. He said, "I only use six to eight inch shiners and they cost a little more. I use big shiners to catch big fish. Is that OK?"

"Heck Yes!" was my answer!

We agreed to meet the very next morning at 6:00 am. He had had a cancellation and I was in. He gave me detailed directions on where to meet him and I was excited.

I carefully laid out everything I was going to need the next day. My fishing shirt (long sleeve), pants (zip off), socks, deck shoes, sun screen, a couple of bottles of water, a chocolate meal bar, camera, and my best fishing hat. I was ready!

I could hardly sleep and the clock moved so slowly I would have sworn it had stopped. Finally the numbers on the clock lit up 5:00 am! I was up and turned off the alarm. Robin did not move from her slumber. I dressed in all of about five minutes and I was ready to be out the door.

It was 5:30 a.m. as I left Robin half asleep. I kissed her good bye and left the information as to where I would be and when I should be returning. Off I went to a local convenience store, where I was to meet my guide for the day. He had made arrangements for me to leave my car there for the day with the manager of the store.

I got there early and bought a large cup of coffee and had a nice conversation with the store manager about the safety of my car. He assured me that he would be there all day so not to worry. He was good friends with the fishing guide and went to church with him on Sundays.

As I drank my coffee, my guide pulled up and off we went in his black pickup truck pulling a bass boat that would turn anyone's eye. It was eighteen glorious feet of metallic red and green fiberglass. It was something I just knew would find fish.

The boat was a piece of art on a trailer. I could see a casting platform, and that it had a center console. It had a huge Black Max Mercury outboard bolted on the transom. It was ready for some action on the water. A smaller trolling motor was affixed to the bow of the boat. Fishing rods were rigged and in their holders. A large landing net was there stored at the side of the console waiting to be used to bring in the monster bass I would catch that day.

If it went as fast as it looked and was able to seek out the big bass, I knew I was in for a great day on the water.

Sammy introduced himself as he came into the store. He was tall and weathered, slim, and the fishing shirt was sun faded, freshly washed, and pressed.

He had on zip-off pants and boat shoes that had seen water but were well taken care of. Not much with words, he was prepared to do business. The owner of the store had his standing order ready, a large cup of coffee and two large bags of ice for the coolers.

We loaded up the coolers with ice, climbed into Sammy's truck, and the excitement started to build. We drove a short way to a privately gated lake with an entrance ramp where we unloaded and were on the water before 6:30 am.

Sammy asked some questions about my fishing background while we loaded the boat and watched the sunrise through the mist over the lake.

It was still hazy and just light as we finished drinking our coffee, sitting in the boat. When it was light enough to take off, we got under way to our first destination. Sammy instructed on how to properly bait the hook with a huge shiner and I cast it to the spot he indicated.

The line was in the water less than a minute when Bam! Fish on! I had a hit and it turned out to be just one of the several six to ten pound bass of the day.

The morning was fantastic. The weather was cool and crisp as the boat flew across the water so fast it would bring tears to your eyes.

My dream was coming to life. Sammy would maneuver us to a spot and rig a line for me. He would tell me where to cast, when to be patient, when to set the hook, and how to reel the fish to the boat so he could slip it into the net.

We would celebrate, take some pictures, and before I knew it he would sing out "Turn your hat around," and we were off to the next spot. We would be off in a flash, up on plane, and skipping over the water to the next spot.

Sammy drove the boat, baited the lines, provided encouragement, and took pictures of each fish I caught with me smiling like I had just been told I would be on stage with John Maxwell and my book was a new best seller.

It was just four hours later with sore arms and a red, sun burnt neck when we happily winched the boat back on the trailer and headed for some ice cold sweet tea.

Sweet tea, of course, is the nectar of the Gods in the South when it is made with the local cane sugar and lots of it, then poured over a huge glass of ice. When we settled, I asked, "So, how is business?"

## Robin's Rhetoric:

*As a child, the only fishing I did was with a cane pole and usually dough balls for bait. I did not eat fish nor did I want to clean them, so fishing was something to pass the time with a friend or my cousin Skip. I really did not care about the catching part.*

*Throughout our marriage, Dick has fished with various friends and our children. On a Saturday morning fishing trip I usually sat in the front of the boat and read magazines, praying I would not get hooked.*

*In recent years, Dick has really enjoyed fly-fishing alone or with local guides in several states. I use the time to hang out at a condominium, explore little shops, sleep in, sit in the sun, or generally take some time alone.*

# CHAPTER 2

# The Question

*"Learn from yesterday, live for today, hope for tomorrow. The important thing is not to stop questioning." —Albert Einstein*

"So, how is business, Sammy?" This is one of my favorite questions to folks that I have done business with or would like to do business with. I always stay ready, looking to learn something new that will help those who come through my door.

His answer was, "Well, I have been a guide for over thirty years and I have learned a few things.

"My business is fishing and fishing is my business! A lot of people think all you have to do is buy a boat, some fishing gear from Walmart, print some business cards, and you're a guide. Man, I wish that were all there was to it. Being a guide takes a lot of time! Years of sweat, practice, investment, and staying on top of the business at hand.

"Catching fish! There is a whole lot you need to do each day before you can take someone out on the water where they can be successful catching fish.

"You have to keep learning and growing. It's like this. Some people are like the pond on the side of the road. Water goes in and stagnates and never goes out. It becomes green with a thick scum on top and no fish or anything else will go or live there after a while.

"Then there are people who are like the lakes around here that have water flowing in, it is shared and flows out. They are crystal clear and fish and every animal, including humans, wants to be there and be a part of it.

"So do you want to be like the pond along the side of the road or the lake where you can see all the way to the bottom?"

## Learning is good—Sharing is better!

"People pay for catching, not for fishing! This year has been somewhat slow and the water is down. Lots of sun and only a little rain usually means you really have to know your craft as a guide to be able to put people in the right place and at the right time to catch fish. My year is always full.

"It seems every year more and more people want to fish with me. My calendar is getting full so at this stage of the game I am teaching my craft to a younger guide who I know will continue to care as much about the fish as the client. So, to answer your question, business is great!"

He continued on saying, "I have spent hours and hours on each lake around here taking time looking at the lake maps, checking the depths and vegetation locations. Sometimes these things change monthly, so you have to always be aware of the surroundings. I have made a lot of notes in my journal and talked to everyone I can about each lake. For each lake I fish I have a journal of notes with times, dates, vegetation, water temperatures, and catches. This has been a lifetime of homework and it never stops or misses a day."

"The first thing I do each day is check the weather. The weather will influence how I make my decisions for the day.

"Once I know the predicted temperature, rain chance, water temperature, water clarity, pollen count, wind, and UV index, I will look at the journals and decide which lake to go to. Next, I look at the best ramp location to put into the lake for shorter runs in the boat and more time fishing for the client. Each fishing time allotment is four hours. You see, the client spends good money with me to catch fish. I know they call it fishing and not catching, but if they don't catch fish and have some pictures to take back home they will not be happy and if they are not happy they won't come back or tell anyone about me.

"If they don't have a good time it won't be good for me or the other guides. It is not just me they are dealing with. It is every other guide who makes a living fishing.

"Now I have to decide which bait we will be using. Some folks like to use live bait and some like artificial. This is a question I always ask when they are on the phone. Do you remember that? I shook my head. If it is live bait, I have to get up earlier and get to the bait shop and hand pick the shiners before the other guides get there. You see, big shiners catch big fish."

Wow, I was really learning now. I had enjoyed a great day on the water but boy I was going to school over a big glass of ice-cold sweet tea.

He said, "Next, is getting the right rod, reel, and setup to ensure the most catches. What you are looking to achieve is having happy clients at the end of the day. Now that is what you are looking for.

"Oh, I almost forgot," he said. "I have to make sure the boat is clean and has been washed from the trip the day before. The cooler needs to be packed with ice and bottled water. I must be sure the gas tanks are filled, the motor is in good working order, and the batteries have been charged and are ready to go.

"Now it is time to pick up the client and go fishing. This is the most important time of the morning. When I pull up and meet the client for the first time I know I am setting the expectations for the day. The truck has to be spotless, both inside and out and the boat has to shine and say, 'I catch fish and go fast!' If I have made all the right decisions and done my homework before we hit the water, all will go well. I always have contingency plans for bad weather—and bad clients.

"Plan B is always a trip to the Bass Pro Shop for lunch and 'fishin' learnin'." Sammy leans back and takes a long slow drink of that ice cold sweet tea, and spits out in a slow and intentional southern drawl, "What did you learn?"

**Robin's Rhetoric:**

> *So much of this book is an evolution of everything we have experienced throughout life. We need to give credit to the years we spent as youth members of Girl Scouts and Boy Scouts and the twenty-five plus years we spent as adult volunteers. Leadership, or our understanding of it, was firmly developed*

*through those experiences. "Be Prepared" is a way of life.*

*In the late 1980s, I was a Cub Scout Day Camp director. Camp operated on Plan B daily. I can't tell you how many projects and activities have been planned and then altered before completion. Plan B is usually ready in the back of my mind. I love the saying, "I plan and God laughs." When we get down to Plan "F" or "G", I start to worry.*

*I try to take care of today, today. Clear up those things lying around that are part of everyday life. It's nice to wake up in the morning and start new.*

# CHAPTER 3

# What Did I Learn?

*"Anyone who stops learning is old, whether at twenty or eighty. Anyone who keeps learning stays young. The greatest thing in life is to keep your mind young." —Henry Ford*

I thought for a few minutes and looked at my notes, which I had taken on the back of the placemat that on the front showed a much younger Sammy holding the biggest bass I had ever seen. He sat quietly waiting to see if the city boy from Clearwater had learned anything from a country boy from Clewiston. Here is what I had written down on that placemat:

To be successful I have to do my homework daily and that is an ongoing and continuous thing. Every day I get up, get dressed, and meet the world head on.

Stephen Covey said, "Begin with the end in mind!"[1] It is what you do daily that will drive your company. It is the homework you do before the client arrives that will make the difference. Take a look at your day planner or "to do" list and make sure you are associating with people who are taking you forward on your journey.

I have to ask the right questions of the clients to be able to set the expectations before we start to work together. I need to have those expectations down in black and white so I can refer to them and make sure that I fulfill my clients' dreams.

Questions are always the start of a great client relationship. Make sure they are written down and

1        Covey, S. (1990). *The 7 Habits of Highly Effective People*. Simon Schuster Ltd Uk.

both you and the client read them and agree on them. Setting the expectations between you and the client will keep your business on calm waters.

I have to keep a good eye on the weather of my community—state, nation, and world. I need to know what things cost, any new procedures, any new practices, what is the cost involved as far as time and commitment, and what the investment will be.

Consistent awareness of what is going on around you keeps your business moving forward. Adjusting to those opportunities will make or break your company. If you skip this step, you will not know how to stay in the competitive market. You could price yourself out or underprice yourself and go out of business.

I should have the right equipment for the job we will be doing and I have to keep up with the latest equipment to stay current.

Do you have the right equipment to do the job and do you know how to skillfully use or apply it for the best outcome? This could mean learning the latest program on the computer, smart phone, digital camera, or social media. If this is not your strong side,

**"Do What YOU Do Best and
Farm Out the Rest." —D.W. Powell**

I have to know how to use each piece of equipment. (More homework.) I will have to investigate and be competent with each piece of equipment needed to do the job.

Investigation of equipment and the knowledge of how it will be used are critical before you purchase. Is a lightweight fly rod and reel needed or do you need a sturdy deep sea rod and reel?

I have to always have a plan B and C to deal with clients and the weather.

Have a plan. Work the plan. Having plans B, C, D, and E will ensure you can find a way to succeed even when conditions change.

Sammy said, "Well done! If you have time for one more glass of that ice cold sweet tea I will explain how clients are like the fish we fish for."

I said, "Let me call my wife." I called Robin and said I would be a little later than I thought and she said she expected that and was down at the pool, reading a book and was looking forward to a date night out at a great restaurant and some entertainment in downtown Orlando!

I said, "Love ya, see you in a while." After forty-two years of marriage, she knew "in a while" will mean a couple of hours. She is patient when she knows I am talking to someone, gathering information we can use for our clients. She also knows that I love to learn and finding mentors has become a habit.

I used up three more placemats and Sammy spoke a whole lot quicker now that he had a serious audience. As Sammy spoke, the other fishing guides were coming in for the day and the table got crowded and Sammy spoke even quicker.

It was amazing that I was accepted by the guides but I was the one taking notes and many of them later asked if I would send them a copy. So, consequently this is just as much for them as it is for you.

I wrote as fast as I could and I will do my best to share what I learned that day at the diner.

## Robin's Rhetoric:

*Dick is a great people person. Thankfully, he also shares much of what he learns with me. We have both learned so much and gleaned priceless bits of knowledge from so many people we have met along life's journey.*

*The important message here is that we have listened and applied this knowledge to our lives and our businesses.*

# CHAPTER 4

# Clients Are Like Fish

*"All clients' needs and expectations are vastly different." —Bruce Bennett*

Sammy said there are four kinds of clients/fish.

They are:

1. Ready to bite

2. Not ready to bite

3. Will never bite

4. Listens, thinks, decides, comes back to eventually bite

## 1. Ready to Bite

These are the fish that are ready to have what you are offering. They know what they want and have already done their homework. They have nibbled and smelled the bait and it's all good! Now is the time to ask questions to insure all of their expectations will be met. The expectations part is huge. If both parties do not agree on what is expected the deal will fall through and trust will be lost. This means that all you have to do is ask some interview questions and then be quiet and take the order. Write it up and reel them in. These clients are landed and netted without a long fight or much involvement. They know what they want and they want it now. After the successful catch and release, make sure to send a hand written note to say "Thank You" for their business. Ask for a testimonial and if it will be OK to use it in your next sales campaign.

Follow up in three to six months to see how they are doing and if they need something or maybe they know someone who needs what you have to offer. Ask for referrals. Don't be shy. They already know you and you have built the "Know, Like, and Trust" with them. Ask them when they are coming back. How can you be of service/value to them? If you don't ask, YOU DON'T GET! Always keep the fresh bait out for them to smell and nibble. Stay in contact! You never know when they will tell their success story to one of their best friends coming your way.

## 2. Not Ready to Bite

These fish are not ready, yet. Present the bait, product, or service. Stop! Listen! Plant the idea. Be QUIET! This fish is a deep thinker and does not make quick decisions. If you present too much or for too long they will be overwhelmed and swim away, never to return. Otherwise, they will come back with questions for you. Answers should be direct and factual. You might very well have to answer them more than once.

They are the ones that like to have the bait changed because the scent is gone. Do your best and move on. Do follow up and send a Thank You note for the meeting.

### 3. Will Never Bite

These fish will take the bait right off the hook over and over. They will ask a hundred questions and you will never be able to answer them all. One question seems to lead to another. They will never be satisfied and always be a problem for you to handle. They will want you to lower the price and devalue yourself to get the job. They are time wasters. This is a game to them and they will suck you into a never ending merry go round conversation. Smile and move away quickly. Learn how to spot these fish quickly, so they don't catch you.

## 4. Will Listen, Think, Decide, and Come Back

These fish want to taste the bait, hear the "What Is in It for Me?!?", and take some time to think about the options. Present the bait. Listen. Plant the idea. Be QUIET! They need quiet and time to consider everything.

Follow UP! This is a fish/client that needs to have a relationship with you. They will be buying you, not your product or service. The product or service will be secondary to you and what you bring to the table. Reel in the fish. Stay by their side. Release gently. After the release send a Thank You card. Ask for referrals and a testimonial. This is the client you will have built a long term relationship with. Although not a fast sale, it will be one that goes on and on.

This person will not be a short-time friend. You will have them for life. Building long-term relationships by providing friendship, service, and customer satisfaction is what your goal should be.

All of a sudden Sammy got up and started out the door. He called back over his shoulder that it was time to get back to work so he could clean and wash the boat and get ready for tomorrow. I thanked him and promised to be back, soon!

WOW! Being schooled in business from a fishing guide!

### Robin's Rhetoric:

*If you think about it, the people you asso-ciate with probably fall into three or four or seven categories—just like the fish. In my business, I have learned to not get excited about a new customer until they are ready to place an order.*

*I have been in partnership with Dick in a cus-tom imprinting and embroidery business for twenty-two years. I used to just wait around* when people told me they were going to order some shirts knowing there were just so many orders I could juggle at one time.

Not anymore. I have no idea how many potential good customers I never knew about because I was waiting and waiting for a "big order" from a friend. Our business has been mostly word of mouth. We specialize in orders under the standard twenty-four pieces.

I knew there would be a time commitment with each order and since I did most of the work, too many jobs at one time would be a problem.

It went like this: Wait for all the elements for an order to be ready to move forward. Hurry up to complete the order. Pray another order did not come in at the same time because *one person could only do so much. I really did not look for work when I was waiting for confirmations for something that was stewing.*

*At some point, I realized that talk was cheap. REAL orders now **start** with the customer's artwork and go no further without an actual order for something to put the artwork on. Customers are like fish and when they are ready, so am I.*

*Meanwhile, I am still open for anything that swims by and wants to do business. I keep my "net" filled with people I meet networking and other opportunities.*

# CHAPTER 5

# Fish Are Like Clients

*"Give your clients the earliest delivery consistent with quality—whatever the inconvenience to us."*
*—Arthur C. Nielson*

## What fish and clients have in common

So what do a fish and a client have in common?

They are both cruising around trying to find something they want but can't quite identify or they are sitting and waiting for something new to swim by.

Every client that I deal with comes to me thinking they either know exactly what they need and want or they have no clue. The thing I have to remember is that they are coming to me because to them I am the expert and so I must actually be an expert.

They are both hungry! They are hungry for information to be able to answer those logical questions in their heads and then to go forward using the feelings that they have by connecting with you. They both want something they don't have!

The most important thing I learned from my friend the guide was that I had to use different baits with different people at different times. One size or type of bait does not fit all.

Clients are like fish. They are always asking the same thing: *"What's In It for Me!"*

Fishing and business both require:

1. Research

2. Prepare

3. Execute

4. Network

5. Celebrate

6. Evaluate

The fishing guide considers the season, weather, water conditions, time of day, licensing, and anything else that might affect the day's fishing.

The guide prepares the boat, the bait, the lines, the reels, and the client for the day. He reviews notes, studies the fishing reports, and uses his knowledge and experience for a good result.

The guide prepares the experience for the client and the client for the experience. He baits the hook and coaches the process of reeling in the fish.

The guide works the net to land the fish. Face it, there is a little finessing involved in just knowing when and how to work that net.

Everyone celebrates each success. It is part of the experience. Enjoy those momentary successes.

After the celebration, evaluate what just happened. The evaluation process should not be overlooked. What was good, what could have been improved? What are you going to do differently next time?

Notice that Sammy kept notes on everything. Every lake, weather condition, water condition, and time of year was recorded. It all documents the experience for future reference and he really does refer back to his notes—every time.

Start with the previous evaluation for anything you do. It helps to not make the same mistakes over and over and perhaps take advantage of previously missed opportunities. Your performance will improve and so will the results.

## Robin's Rhetoric:

*When my customers are ready to get down to business they have either a good idea or actual artwork ready. They know what they want, how many, and are ready to make decisions.*

*They often have done some research about me and my product line. Today, everything is on the Internet. Good customers do some research and are better informed every year. They understand what they can expect from me. I have listened to their criteria and tried to fit my capabilities to their expectations.*

*Most of my current customers come through business networking. This platform allows me to educate my fellow networkers as my sales force.*

*A celebration comes with each satisfied customer.*

*I find the evaluation step a part of living. Did the finished project look as expected? Should anything be improved on the re-order?*

# Section II

The hope is that this book has meaning for you and you will read it more than once.

**Please be encouraged to <u>write in the book</u>! Take Notes!**

Remember to check back periodically and see how you are doing or adjust your plans.

You might even change from pencil to ink of different colors each time you review your plans.

To obtain a Complimentary Workbook, go to: www.EWFW.org/.

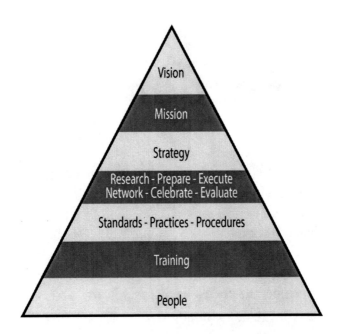

# CHAPTER 6

# Business

*"Business, more than any other occupation, is a continual dealing with the future; it is a continual calculation, an instinctive exercise in foresight." —Henry R. Luce*

Business and Fishing are the art of:

1. Research

2. Prepare

3. Execute

4. Network

5. Celebrate

6. Evaluate

# 1. Research

They call it fishing, not catching for a reason. Sometimes you have to do a whole lot of fishing to get a little catching. Research is the key to successful catching. Research happens daily and the learning that is applied will take you where you need to be at the right time. The trick is to do a little research and learn a little every day. Do a little more research and learn a little more.

1. Who: Who are the fish?

2. What: What do you have to offer?

3. Where: Where is the target area?

4. When: When is the best date and time?

5. How: How to make the presentation?

6. Weather: What are the "weather conditions" in their world?

**Who: Who are the fish?**

This is a question to spend some time with. Who you are going after will tailor the rest of the decisions. What is the age demographic? What is the mean income bracket? What do they do for a living? What do they do for fun? Be specific. Fishermen do not fish for bass and salmon at the same time. Who are you looking for?

Just an idea:

*Young upper middle class professionals between the ages of 25 and 35 with an income of over 100K who are interested in extreme sports, located in the Atlanta area.*

The "What's in it for me?" (WIIFM) is as important as the product or service you are offering.

They need to know the WHY. Why should I bite/ buy what you have?

There are seven learning styles that are good to know when you are dealing with people and with fish.

These are a few of the fish we have encountered in our quest of the perfect fish:

- Pike
- Bass
- Gar
- Bluegill
- Catfish
- Rainbow Trout
- Carp

**Pike**—Flashy! They wear only the latest clothes and styles. They will display a lot of bling. Their vehicle is shinny and new. It will have all of the extras. When you pick up a Pike the first thing you notice is the teeth. They have lots of teeth (or dollars) to grab what they want and hold on. They eat when they believe everything is in their favor.

Pike are inter-personal. They are sensitive to moods, temperament, and feelings of others. They normally have professions and are leaders, people who work in care-giving professions. They make good team members. When speaking with them, they like team-building exercises, working with others, and talking about learning.

**Bass**—Noticeable for their large mouths and ability to take in large bites of bait and information at one time. They are also loud mouths. They will want to show their great knowledge and skill at making you look small. The really good part of working with a bass is that once they make their minds up, it's all over. They will attack the bait and the fight will be on. They eat only when they are ready. Don't push them too hard or they will swim away.

Bass are intrapersonal. They are sensitive to their own moods, feelings, and reactions. They are normally therapists, their patients, or writers who reflect on their own experiences. They like to work independently and spend time on their own in order to reflect on new experiences.

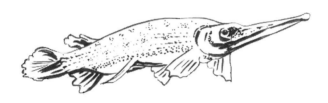

**Gar**—Move fast and are sleek hunters. They grow to huge sizes because when they see something they want they go after it. They are always on the hunt for food or a good deal, a new toy, or new product. They eat whatever they can hunt down and ambush. Be very careful with your fingers if you get too close.

The Gar is logical, mathematical, and sequential. These people have the ability to symbolize relationships, to calculate, and to test theory with reality. They are scientists, mathematicians, and computer programmers. They can formulate new concepts and are aware their ideas and designs must work in the real world.

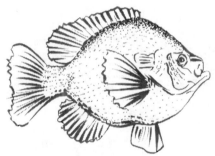

**Bluegill**—They like only one or two choices in baits. When they are hungry they eat. When they are not hungry they can be enticed to eat if you have the bait they are looking for. Do you have what they are looking for ready to dangle in front of them?

Bluegills are musical. These are people who are sensitive to sound and pitch and have the ability to express emotion through sounds. They like to use background music and make up tunes to help in the learning process.

**Catfish**—When I think of the catfish, I remember the long whiskers that make them look wise beyond their years. They can grow to be several feet long and they are bottom feeders. They eat anything and everything they find. They will be cautious and testing your knowledge of your product or service. They will want to know all the facts and see the charts and graphs. They are slower and shyer in finding the bait, but once they do hold on, they are in. Don't pull too hard!

Catfish are kinesthetic. These people like the ability to use the body in work, sports, and artistic expression. They will be dancers, athletes, skilled technicians, and crafts people who use tools. They have trouble sitting still. They will develop a skill by practicing it.

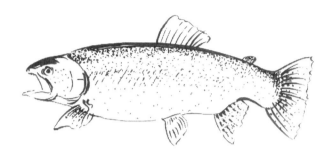

**Rainbow Trout**—These are the fish/clients that I love the most. They are small and beautiful. They sip the insects from the top of the water surface. They are patient hunters. When they see what they want they like to surge up and ambush their prey. They might be small but they are mighty. Don't be fooled by beauty. Keep an eye on them. They are in it to win it.

Rainbow trout are linguistic. Words matter. These people are sensitive to words, their meaning, and order within a sentence. They will be poets, writers, politicians, and lawyers. They like to explain using words both written and spoken.

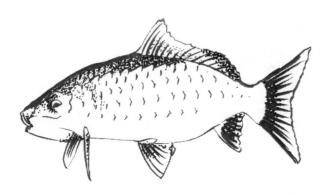

**Carp**—Live a long time by being able to recognize a good deal and a bad meal. They are very personable and will stay calm and listen intently. They will gather all the information before making a choice.

Carp are Spatial. These people have the ability to perceive and reproduce shapes and their placement, even in the absence of solid examples. They would include painters, sculptors, designers, architects, navigators, air-traffic controllers, and carpenters. They like the use of color, pictures, designs, graphs, and charts.

## What: What do you have to offer?

What do you have to offer that is different or unique? This is a point on which to spend some time and have a good answer. What is the value you bring? Do you do it differently? How? Do you have a strange and different hook? Is it quicker, faster, and can jump higher or will it make life easier, make me more money and provide an exciting life? Example: "We at Big Daddy's Crayfish Farm always count in a baker's dozen." Every fish you encounter has different likes and dislikes. They will change by the minute. The water, the time of day, and the weather conditions surrounding them affects what they will do.

## Where: Where is the target area?

Once you have decided on the "who" and the "what", decide on the "where." Stake it out. Learn everything you can about it. Where do the successful people meet? Where do they go for fun? What do they do for fun? What kind of businesses are in the area. Be the "go to" person that has the information about the area. Keep informed about the local and surrounding businesses, restaurants, coffee shops, attractions, hotels, car rentals, services, and more. Keep a good list of all the people you know, like, and trust that you are already doing business with in the area.

Are we fishing shallow or deep water? Shallow water is where the small fish live and are caught. Minnows are easy to catch with some bread spread over the surface of the lake. Bream are at a different depth as well as the bass. Each has its own comfort level in the water. You need to make an intentional decision as to where and at what depth you wish to fish. What are you expecting to catch? Be sure to fish where the fish you are trying to catch spend their time.

It takes a lot of small fish to fill the bucket. The deep water is where the big fish are. It only takes a few big fish to fill the bucket. The object is to have more big fish than small fish. Work smart, not hard.

Are you looking for those that hang out on the surface or those that like it deep? Where are the fish you want to catch?

## When: When is the best date & time?

Looking at the tide charts and the moon phases will help when fishing. The time of day depends on if the client is a morning, afternoon, or an after-hours person. The date always revolves around the day of the week that is best for them. Not you! *The Wall Street Journal* provides a balanced, unbiased view of business and the world six days a week. Use your day planner and provide a date and time to meet the client. Only provide two choices. Knowing when to fish is a large part of the homework.

Cable news, financial programs, and being in tune with the business climate in your area add to the "when."

When you fish is as important as who, what, or where. Be sensitive to the timing.

## How: How to make the presentation?

Some days a quick retrieval will result in a bite, on others a slow troll is needed, and still on others an almost silent approach will be needed. You need to know the fish well enough to decide how flashy or reserved to act.

Body language is 80 percent of communication. Pay attention and be sensitive to the posturing, fidgeting, finger tapping. Take the clues and alter the presentation accordingly. Your own body language is also a huge factor. What is the message being sent before you speak? What are you wearing? In fishing this is called matching the hatch. I might wear a suit and tie to a formal business meeting and a golf shirt if we are playing golf. Men, don't show the hairy chest. No one wants to see it. Cologne, it is true a little dab will do you. Women, dress as if your grandpa was the client. Perfume is great if only the wearer can enjoy it. Be on time or a little early. Stand tall and be in the moment. Keep your hands out of your pockets. It is OK to use hand gestures, but do not act like you are waving down a passing car. Communication is intentional and a give and take. Be in the moment. Look in a mirror before going out. This gets easier with practice.

## Weather: What are the "weather conditions" in their world?

Knowing how hard the wind is blowing and from which direction will help you know how to speak the right words at the right time. A storm on the horizon or sunny skies affect the overall outcome. Make sure you know what is happening in the local community as well as in the nation and the world.

Take a few minutes and get to know a little about them. Something major may be going on in their lives. If something is happening to them, their family, or friends, this is not a good time to sell. It is a good time to listen. Ask a few questions at the beginning and alter the presentation as needed.

Many successful relationships begin with getting to know how the "wind is blowing" or if it is warm or cool. Use the FORM method at the first meeting.

## F – Family

This is all about building the relationship. Most people love talking about their children, significant others, and someone special in their lives.

## O – Occupation

Humans seem to gather around others who are involved in the same career, job, or desire to change their occupations. Find a common ground and listen.

## R – Recreation

This is my normal opening question: What do you like to do for fun? Everyone has something they like to do. Sports, outdoors, TV, bike riding, bird watching, boating, etc.

## M – Matter (things that matter to them)

What matters most to them? Most people will say their family. Ask for them to list the most important things. This could turn out to be their value system and give you an insight and a relationship builder.

# 2. Prepare

You have to do the homework which will prepare you for the opportunity when it arises. Cast your bait everywhere and often. There is a real difference between selling, telling, and having a passion for what you are doing.

Selling is seen as not being prepared and as a good friend of mine says, "Showing Up and Throwing Up." Slick salesmen have a reputation for selling things to us we don't really need or want. This creates mistrust and ill will. When this happens the proposed client will likely tell everyone around them of the experience. It will take a long time to correct this reputation. Good business practices go beyond that and you should only be selling things people need or truly want. You are looking for repeat customers, not customers who run the other way the next time they see you.

Telling a story is a little better. At least you have learned enough about your product to explain it in a few short and sweet sentences. Find an experience that you can relate to the client. Build a bond between you. Use your story and not someone else's. When it is not authentic the client will see right through it. You cannot claim what you have not done. If you use someone else's story, make sure you start out that way. Don't lose the trust of the person you are taking to by telling a story that you do not own. Be concise. Be truthful. Be real.

When you can tell the story and your passion for what you do and have to share shows through, this will take you where you want to go. When you are speaking from your passion the person you are talking to will be able to see it in your posture as well as in your voice. There is nothing worse than a story seller who does not believe in or have the passion for what they are sharing. Whatever it is, it is never ever all about the money. It is about the person.

## Practice—Practice—Practice

I cannot say this enough. Everywhere you go during your normal day you will meet people who can use your product or know someone who needs it. If you do not have a thirty or sixty second speech with a tag line, you need to create one! If you don't know how then go to: www.EWFW.org and get your Complementary Workbook. If you are having trouble with creating your 30 second speech, email us and let us help you create one that will work for you. Practice in front of a mirror and then on family and friends.

Remember you will need to say everything in thirty to sixty seconds. The opening begins with your name (Dick Powell) and your company name (Earth Wind Fire Water Training and Development)—this should take eight seconds. Time it!

The middle is for what makes you and your company unique, (We build better leaders.) and why they should give you more time. (You will learn to execute and win the sale every time.) Finish with your name, (Dick Powell), company name, (Earth Wind Fire Water Training and Development), and a catchy tag line (IF you're not developing yourself—who else will?).

Find a mirror. Post your short speech on the mirror in the bathroom. Practice it while you are combing your hair, brushing your teeth, and if you are a guy, shaving. Write it down repeatedly. The more you write it and say it the more it will be part of your normal speech pattern. If while saying it you stumble over a word, change the word so you are comfortable with the flow. It should sound smooth like your normal speech pattern. Find a friend or a group of friends and "cast" it to them.

If they are good friends, they will tell you if it needs improvement and they can help you create something better. Take some time in the creating. Successful business minded people take a lot of time and spend a lot of money on these "commercials." Get it right for you.

It should take you longer than twenty minutes and a glass of wine to create yours. Make it work for you personally. This is the hard part. What sounds good and works for me will not sound good and work for you. You must own the words and the meaning of the words.

Keep it concise and clear. Thirty seconds or less! Time it. People will stop listening to you after sixty seconds or the first "And um," They will mentally move on unless they hear a reason to pay attention longer or make an appointment to learn more. Remember that too short is just as bad as too long.

If they are interested, get their information to follow up and set an appointment. I carry some three by five inch colored index cards to gather information. You will need to note their names, phone numbers (both cell and office), email, spouse, children, and even pets. Get as much as you can. Write it in your own handwriting so you can read it later when you are doing your follow ups. People love it when they see you taking notes. It means you care enough about them to take a genuine interest in them, to be prepared and ready to do business. Keep doing it!

Keep track of the card or wherever you wrote the information. The card shows you care enough to want to remember them. They will also remember giving you the same information numerous times if you keep asking the same questions every time you meet. Have a way to keep the cards handy so you can refer to them in the future.

Everywhere you go you are going to see and talk to people. It will feel a little weird at first. It will be better over time as you practice and become fluent in this skill. Practice makes permanent, so develop a system that works for you and use it, every time.

## Gear

Business cards are your best reference to leave behind. You should not give one unless you receive one in return. If they do not have a card whip out one of your three by five cards and use it. Business cards need to be where you can reach them and never have to search for them. Put them in the same pocket or location in your purse every day when you get dressed.

Business cards are now being replaced by QR codes that will allow any smart phone to take them directly to your website. Use this service just like a business card. Give yours and get theirs.

I use three by five index cards for notes. They have lines to keep things straight and have more room to write notes than business cards. I like the colored ones and I use different colors for different events. That way when I am back at the office doing the follow up, I know where I met the person I am calling. There is room to add more notes for future reference. My wife uses her trusty date stamper to track when she contacts people. It fits on the lines and saves time.

Pens can be uncertain and pencil points break. Have several stashed in brief cases, cars, iPad cases, etc. You never know when yours will die or when the other person will not have one and you will be the hero. The pens and pencils may have your information on them or not. If you are using pens as advertisement make sure they are a good quality, not necessarily more costly. They do not have to be expensive to work, but make sure they work.

A note pad for 'notes to self' is another good way to follow up. When someone is talking with me I am always taking notes. There are two reasons:

**One**—people will feel special when they see you are taking notes.

**Two**—I sometimes forget where and when I met you and what you do. I take notes. I date the notes. I keep them where I can access them as needed.

Name badges and logo shirts are easy ways to be your own billboard. If you choose a name badge, make the name large enough to read from four to six feet away. It should be placed on the upper right side of your coat, shirt, or blouse. Ladies, place it high so eyes stay where they should be, on your eyes.

If you are wearing a logo shirt, hat, etc. make sure the logo depicts **your** business or includes the business name. Make sure your logo can be printed as well as embroidered. There are logos that will look great on paper and will not transfer well to embroidery. It is best to check first with someone in the imprinting business before you spend any money or sign a contract. It is a great way to promote who you are or what you do and often opens a conversation.

If you are creating a new logo, be sure to test market it among your worst critics and best cheer-leaders. You will get a good cross section of what emotions are evoked and what people will think when they see it. A graphic artist should give you a few options to choose from. Each medium will have different characteristics. Make sure it will work for any future applications. Brand your-self so people remember what you do. Branding is the emotion people feel when they see your brand. There are commercials that we all recog-nize quickly just by the logo. People remember the brand logo first before they remember you. When they can hook them together that is when you have a winner

# 3. Execute

## The Presentation: Be Prepared

**Music:** Listen to inspirational music on the way to the meeting or presentation. Sometimes I listen to upbeat, fast music to get my head in the game. Other times I listen to motivational speakers like Zig Ziglar, Stephen Covey, or John Maxwell. This helps me get in the right mind set to be a successful business person.

**Dress:** The subject of what to wear needs to be visited and revisited. Do I send the message I want to be sending by what I am wearing? Is what I am wearing right for the occasion? Do I dress like the person I want to be? This is the question I ask myself every time I get ready to meet a client.

I have learned the hard way that just because I am the owner of the business does not mean I can show up in anything I like. One, it does not show respect to you or the client. Two, you are there to do business. Three, how you present yourself will set the tone of the interaction. Four, your employees will dress like you do.

Will you be meeting in the boardroom or the locker room? Sandals and shorts for guys will not cut it for a good first impression. Even in Florida, for the most part, I am in business attire. A dress shirt, tie (if called for), dress pants, socks, and polished shoes. Sometimes a dress shirt and newer jeans—pressed, starched, and creased are more appropriate. Do your homework. It is better to overdress where we live. You are there to do business, so arrive ready to do business.

When the relationship is solid and sandals and shorts are the dress of the day, okay! It is better to overdress and remove a tie than to be under dressed and be embarrassed and possibly lose a client.

Match the hatch, as my fly fishing guides would say! This means if I am meeting a client at a fishing boat, dress for fishing. Sailing requires deck shoes and fishing requires wading shoes.

> *"They expect a professional presentation,*
> *so they expect to see a 'Professional'.*
> *"Dress appropriately, but don't be*
> *one of the crowd!" —Wess Roberts*

## Client Information: Do your homework.

Do you remember the notes you took on their business cards or the notes you made in your journal. Use them when you are back at your desk in the office. Check the social media like LinkedIn, Facebook, etc. Ask questions of other people in the area. Do they like sports or hate sports? Do they like dogs or cats, fishing or hunting, bird watching or bird raising? What are their favorite vacation spots, activities, etc.? These conversation starters let the "fish" talk. This is also where relationships are being built.

**Handouts:** If you need them, create them and have them printed by a professional printer if what comes off of your ink jet does not look very professional. Keep publications colorful, short and sweet, and make your points clearly. Less is better than more when it comes to words and paper.

## KISS (Keep It Simple, Sweetheart)

**Know how to spin a yarn:** In sales or with clients, Facts Tell—Stories SELL! Knowing how to tell the story is important. If the story is too long it will be boring. Too short and they won't receive the message you are sending. Make sure they get the point, so repeat the important parts.

## Think it out! Write it out! Shout it out!

Think it out! Your story needs a beginning, a middle, and a conclusion. The beginning will be about you. Who you are, your background, and why you do what you do. The middle is about the value of the product or service and the conclusion will be the what's in it for them or the moral of the story.

Write it out! You will need to do this more than once to iron out all the kinks. Share the written copy with a trusted advisor and then rewrite. I have never known a great story-teller that only writes it down once. The more you write it down the more it will stick to your memory and the words will flow more smoothly.

<u>Know when to be silent</u>:

This is always hard when you are excited to share your passion with others. The problem here is that for some what they will hear is: He showed up and threw up! They say silence is golden. Do not be afraid to just take some quiet time to think, assess the situation, and make good decisions.

## <u>Know when to stop—look—listen—wait</u>.

**Stop!** When you feel the client is tired of listening to you, **stop talking.** Use clear and concise statements just one time. Use enough words to make your points and remember adult attention spans are about eight minutes so keep your side to around five minutes then let the other person talk. Don't keep changing the bait just because it smells good to you.

**Look!** Look for body clues like folded arms, looking down, and the tapping of fingers or jiggling a foot. If the client is not paying attention, stop talking.

**Listen!** Listen to what they want and what they say. What are they looking for? How can you provide that service or product? How can you add value to their life?

**Wait!** Wait for them to ask questions.

<u>Hook & Land</u>: Set the hook and reel them in! You have done the job!

# 4. Network

Your network will be part of your sales and marketing campaign. Join a group of like-minded people that are interested in sharing business, connecting clients, and providing referrals. There are many in your local area that can be of great service to you and your company. Consider the other members as your sales force and remember you are part of theirs. Also, remember it sometimes takes time to develop relationships among the other members. Treat them like clients while teaching them how to provide you referrals.

Go to the Internet and type in "networking groups" and you will have a huge list. If you do not come up with any that will suit you, build your own.

Networking is never about a once a week meeting with friends and other business owners. It is a twenty-four hour, three hundred sixty five day event. Standing in line at the store and you have your company name badge on and someone asks: What do you do? That is an opening! You're at a sporting event and have your company logo shirt on and someone says: What does that stand for? That is an opening! Be intentional and be aware of your surroundings. Someone is always near and ready to hear what you have to offer.

To be a good networker:

1. Have a 30 second description of your company ready at any time.

    a. Opening: Your name and your company's name. Do not add extraneous words. Start with your name, not the twentieth "Hello" or "Good morning." Mine opens with, "Dick Powell, Earth Wind Fire Water Training and Development."

b. Middle: What value do you bring? A few words about what you do. "We provide inspiring accountability and leadership instruction to companies, increase value to their clients and employees, and enhance company growth potential."

c. Ending: Your name, company name, and tag line if you have one: "Dick Powell, Earth Wind Fire Water Training and Development. If you're not developing yourself, who will?"

2. Exchange business cards

a. Take notes

i. Where you met (event/coffee house)

ii. Date/time

b. Record information on the back

c. Follow up within 24 hours

3. Marketing materials

   a. A professional quality tri-fold or other brochure is good to leave with your group so they can share them with potential referrals.

   b. Advertising specialty products are useful but not necessary.

4. Meetings

   a. Show up early.

   b. Dress properly.

   c. It will be all about them.

   d. Do NOT—"Show Up and Throw Up." Present basic information. You are networking to expand your sales force. Leave something to talk about later.

   e. Set up "one-on-ones" with new people you meet to get to know each other and your prospective businesses.

    f. Meet with people outside of regular meetings to keep informed about their businesses.

5. Follow up

    a. Send a card.

    b. Make a phone call.

    c. Send an email.

    d. Meet with people in addition to regular meetings to keep informed about their businesses.

    e. Do follow up. The fortune is in the follow up.

6. Relationships

    a. Good ones develop over time.

    b. All are based on "Know, Like, & Trust", on both sides.

    c. Make a point once a week to do something to expand one relationship.

7. Be in the right spot at the right time.

8. Get out of the office. You grow by getting out, meeting, and greeting others.

9. Get out and about. Some of my best clients were just in line waiting to have someone come up to them and start a conversation. Start with a smile and "Hello."

*"If you are not being seen and heard—You are not being seen and heard!" —Dick Powell.*

# 5. Celebrate

The pros celebrate a win. When you celebrate, you plant deep in your mind the "I did it!" and the "I will do it again!" thought processes. This will keep you going when things get slow or you are struggling to fill the client list. This does not mean go out and buy a new boat! It does not have to cost a dime. It could be a high five with a partner or another cold glass of ice cold sweet tea. Maybe do your own happy dance or eat a favorite celebratory candy bar. The point is to do it and fill your mind with a winner's mind set. The pros celebrate a loss. Learn from what did not go well and you will celebrate more wins than losses. The deal about celebrating the loss is that a loss is not a failure. It is a learning tool when you choose it to be. Celebrate!!

Enjoy the landing, weighing, taking some pictures, cleaning, and eating the big catch!

*"You have to have confidence in your ability and then be tough enough to follow through!"*
*—Rosalyn Carter*

# 6. Evaluate

Every great fisherman I know writes notes back at the dock or office. Let the evaluations dictate how you are going to improve. Be honest with yourself and consider the source of criticisms. We keep a Lessons Learned book on the desk at the office. It is filled with things that went well and those that went not so well. When it is reviewed before a new project we catch some things that we need to change, add, and keep.

**Research:**

<u>Who</u>: What kind of fish was caught?

<u>What</u>: What bait was used?

<u>Where</u>: Where did the catch take place?

<u>When</u>: What was the date and time of the catch?

<u>Weather</u>: Wind speed, Water Temp., cloud cover

**Prepare:** Did I prepare properly?

<u>Practice</u>: Have I practiced enough? What parts need more?

<u>Gear</u>: Did we use the right stuff?

**Execute:**

Presentation

Know how to spin a yarn

Know how to tell a story

Know when to be silent

Hook & Land

**Network:**

Do it daily and it will become a habit.

Let your passion for what you do and the value you bring be heard, seen, and recognized.

## Follow Up—Follow Up—Follow Up

**Celebrate:**

Do it every time!

Be consistent!

**Evaluate:**

What went well?

What could I change?

Is there something I need to add?

What's next?

# No Matter How YOU Feel— Get Up, Dress Up, and Show Up with a Smile on your face.

# Next Steps

**Universal Call to Action**

All of us who are in business or want to be in business must keep learning and growing in the adventure of owning our own profitable business. We need to be constantly aware of what is happening and what is new in the business right now, as well as looking ahead to the future. Learning is not a once in a lifetime action. It is a continuous lifelong endeavor. Once the adventure has started, it is never ending. Evaluate and learn daily.

**Here is my Call to Action:**

My call to action is to be continually excited about learning everything there is to know about the business of being in business and then sharing that knowledge through books, trainings, seminars, and personal interactions. The creation of this book has transformed me from the role of a back seat driver to taking the wheel and sharing my knowledge of the business of business, writing and teaching others the process from the beginning concept on a napkin to the completion and the legacy left for those who will follow.

**Your next step to the Adventure of Business:**

1. Download your Complimentary Workbook for *free* from www.EWFW.org.

2. Complete the homework designing yourself and your company.

3. Set an appointment with Dick by going to: www.EWFW.org

If you are serious about
success in business,
Do It Right Now!

Before you go fishing!!

http://www.ewfw.org

# Acknowledgements

Creating this book has been a long journey. Without the support and encouragement from many people, it could have never happened.

I owe great appreciation and gratitude to my wife of forty years for being with me on this long journey of self-discovery and her belief in me that this is what I was called to do and should be doing as a career.

I owe a lot of thanks to all of the business owners I have had the privilege to interview, learn from, be mentored by, and who encouraged me to share what I have learned with as many people as I can.

# Acknowledgements

This book is dedicated to everyone that I have had the pleasure of spending the day with on the water or learning how to make a business thrive. Thank You!

To Robin, my wife, for sitting through all of the speeches and courses and the many hours of writing and correcting the words I used.

To Kimber, our daughter, who is always believing in my dream and pushing me onward.

To all the friends who find our errors and gently let us know about them.

To Ginger Marks, my publisher, who understood how to correct, encourage, and hold my hand when needed.

To Philip Marks, my editor who took my words and made them make sense, all the while ensuring it was written in my words and thoughts.

To Beverly Womack, a good friend and artist who always comes through with what we need, even before we need it. She is a worldwide calligraphy artist of the highest caliber.

# About the Author

Dick W. Powell grew up in Largo, Florida on a dead-end street which ended in a swamp. He finished high school and worked for General Telephone Company where he began as a lineman and worked his way up to retire after thirty years as the Interim Director of Outside Plant Instruction.

He then went on to build several successful companies as well as becoming a spokesperson for a large manufacturing company located in northern California. It was here that he discovered that what he had always done was what he was supposed to do—help others help themselves to realize their dreams.

Dick is a Certified Life Purpose and Business Coach. He trained with the Life Purpose Institute. He is also a Certified Speaker, Teacher, Coach, and a Founding Partner with the John C. Maxwell Group.

# Other Books by D.W. Powell

*Soar 2 Success With Coaching Skills*—52 Tips to Empower Others and Becoming a Leader in Your Organization *with Elizabeth McCormick*

*Watch for additional books and resources coming soon from Earth, Wind, Fire, Water Training & Development*

*http://www.ewfw.org*

CPSIA information can be obtained at www.ICGtesting.com
Printed in the USA
BVOW04s1335010415

394239BV00009B/51/P